THIS BOOK is to
commemorate the issuance of the
Kickapoo medal
April 5, 1975
and is limited to 15,000 copies
No. 10225

Courtesy of George R. Nielsen

RHONDA DAUGOMAH, *Pam E Tha Quah*, in traditional garments.

THE
KICKAPOO
PEOPLE

by George R. Nielsen

Scientific Editor: Henry F. Dobyns
General Editor: John I. Griffin

PUBLISHED BY INDIAN TRIBAL SERIES / PHOENIX

ABOUT THE TRIBAL CHAIRMAN

Orval L. Kirk, a full-blood Kickapoo, was elected to the position of tribal chairman in June, 1971. To the administration of tribal affairs, he has brought a broad and lengthy experience with the contemporary world.

His early years were in many ways typical of his generation of Kickapoo youth. Even though he was exposed to the older ways by his family that included a grandmother who migrated to Mexico during the Civil War and was returned to Indian Territory by the United States Army, he was enrolled in elementary school at nearby McLoud. Following graduation from high school, during which time he played four years of varsity baseball and basketball, he served in the Navy from 1955 to 1960. In addition to sailing on the *U.S.S. WASP*, he continued his education in service schools and correspondence courses. Ten years after his discharge from the Navy, he received the A.A. degree in accounting from Cerritos Junior College, Norwalk, California. Included among the positions he has held was that of tax representative for the State of California, and just prior to his election as tribal chairman, that of purchasing agent for Worthington Pump in Shawnee, Oklahoma.

During his four year term as chairman, Mr. Kirk has greatly expanded Kickapoo involvement in government programs and projects to improve services for members of the tribe. He has also been active in the Central Tribes of the Shawnee Area (CTSA), a body for the coordinating of Native American activities.

ORVAL L. KIRK, Tribal Chairman of the Kickapoo Nation.

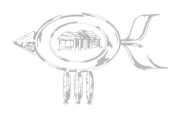

INTRODUCTION

"God is my captain — the world my camping ground, and I am at liberty to go where I choose." This philosophy not only justified the decision of a Kickapoo chief to remain in Mexico in 1868 but conveniently summarizes a reasonable view of the Kickapoo people throughout their history. Distance and space, to the Kickapoo, were not barriers, and compared to the host of nomadic tribes, the Kickapoo were among the most freewheeling. Much of their migration and relocation was not of their own choice, but constituted a response to the pressures of other Indian tribes, European traders, and American settlers. In other instances the decision was arrived at more independently as they sought better hunting grounds or increased isolation from the whites. Even before contact with Europeans, the Kickapoo were evidently mobile, at least

1

within a given range, because their name itself means "he moves about, standing now here, now there." This history is intended to relate both the frequent geographic migrations of the Kickapoo from their homeland in Wisconsin to Mexico, over 1,000 miles away, and also their cultural travels from the seventeenth century into the twentieth.

An Indian historian, Angie Debo, considers the Kickapoo to be the most culturally conservative of Indian tribes. In the fight to maintain their culture, the tribesmen were not isolated in some corner of the desert where they were ignored, but they lived on the cutting-edge of European contact where preservation of their way of life required a constant and conscious effort. From the time of the first contacts with the European, the Kickapoo resisted efforts to convert them by the missionaries, attempts to enroll their children in schools, and pressures to transform them into commercial farmers. Europeans often mistook for arrogance pride of the Kickapoo in his culture and consequent tribal coolness toward European ways. The tenacity Kickapoo demonstrated in retaining their way of life, nevertheless, was more than pride or conservatism, it was a religious conviction. They ardently believed that if they were to give up their ways, the world would come to an end. Time after time they withdrew to an area where they hoped to be left alone, but they could never completely isolate themselves. They never escaped the European presence, but even today they still retain much of their tradition.

2

Kickapoo pride and self-respect also made them feared warriors. Although the total population of the tribe never exceeded 3,000, and the Kickapoo were never as numerous as the Comanche and the Iroquois, they gained the respect of tribal enemy and European alike. No matter where the Kickapoo resided at a given time, his impact was much greater than the size of the tribe warranted. Already in 1710 Antoine Denis Raudot wrote that the Kickapoo were "almost all crippled with wounds and covered with scars, being always at war." Randolph B. Marcy in 1852 believed that "there were no better hunters or warriors upon the border," and that the Kickapoo were not afraid of engaging the plains tribes in battle "provided the odds were not more than six to one against them." The Kickapoo were no more interested in war than was any other nation but our view of the tribe is focused only on the period when the fur trade set the stage for inter-tribal war or when the white men coveted Kickapoo land for farming. In this context of conquest, pillage, and revenge, however, the Kickapoo more than held his own.

The first recorded homeland, reported in the 1650's by French explorers, was in southern Wisconsin along the Fox and Wisconsin Rivers. Here the Kickapoo spent their summers in fixed villages tending their crops. During the winter, however, they roamed south into Illinois looking for game. Prior to the time of the French explorers, the Kickapoo probably lived further east in southern Michigan and began their migration into Wisconsin as Iroquois

3

warriors pushed westward armed with European weapons.

The Kickapoo were people neither of the plain nor the forest, but occupied a transitional zone between the prairie on the west and the deciduous forest on the east. The highlands of this transitional zone nourished a lush grassland while the valleys and stream banks supported heavy growths of trees. Throughout the wanderings of the tribesmen from Wisconsin toward the southwest, they remained in the environment that provided a blend of both types of vegetation. There was a significant difference in temperatures between Wisconsin and Mexico as well as variations in rainfall, but the Kickapoo liked a balance between prairies and forest.

Linguistically the Kickapoo were Algonquian and spoke a language most similar to the Sac and Shawnee, although socially they lived in villages with the Mascouten and Fox. The Kickapoo have been classified as woodland tribes, a group which included the Chippewa, Winnebago, and Potawatomi, yet they did not rely on the wild rice or utilize the canoe as did these neighbors to the north and east. The Kickapoo probably were recent migrants into the south Wisconsin area and had not geared their economy to wild rice. They may have decided against working with the rice that required binding the plant, protecting it from fowl, and harvesting it in canoes.

Like the Fox and Miami, the Kickapoo lived instead by hunting, horticulture, and gathering. The game they sought included deer and bear, which was

4

generally hunted in winter with dogs. Also important was the bison of the prairie which they hunted in summer when the entire village participated. They utilized the surround or set fires that frightened the buffalo toward the waiting hunters. After the crops were harvested, the Indians went south for the winter hunt for three months and returned in early spring to plant their crops. During this early season they lived off the meat and the corn they had dried and hidden the previous fall. The crops they planted were the traditional Indian crops of corn, squash, and beans. They also fished and gathered roots and berries to supplement their diet.

The Kickapoo built separate oval-shaped homes for both winter and summer and located them amidst the trees. Both structures were supported with a green sapling framework, although the summer home was covered with bark of elm or birch while the winter home was covered with mats made of cattails. The floor of the winter house was covered with grass and reed mats for warmth. The summer home was bare or covered only with reed mats, but included a platform along the inside wall of the structure that served as a place to sit or sleep. In more recent times the usual size of the building was sixteen feet in length, twelve feet in width, and ten feet in height. A description of a home on the Wabash River in 1810 stated that the structure was fifty feet long and thirty feet wide. The door always faced east and was covered with a hide. Inside the home was a place for the fire and a hole in the roof above it for the

5

smoke to escape. Over the fire there was generally a pot of food being prepared, the meat and vegetables being simply boiled together into a stew.

Kickapoo handicrafts generally utilized wood and the craftsmen produced functional objects. Among the many necessary items utilized in daily life were cradleboards, large ladles for dipping into the steaming pot of food, bowls, deer calls, and traps. Although the Kickapoo are not considered noteworthy artists, their equipment and utensils were often ornamented with carvings and porcupine quills.

The cycle of Kickapoo festivals and celebrations began in early spring when the first thunder was heard. This tradition was carried into Mexico where the spring arrived earlier, so the festivals often began in February. The coming of spring also signaled the preparation of the summer house and the ritual of opening and renewing the sacred medicine bundles. After a month or so of celebrations that emphasized community association, personal and family feasts were staged for such events as naming babies and commemorating the recent death of a family member. In July or August the villagers were again called together for a corn dance. The dancers wore ceremonial dress and each carried an object, such as a bird's wing, which they waved to the rhythm of the drums. In the fall of the year, the winter homes were prepared, the bundles were tied up, and activity again centered around the family. Winter was the time for hunting, survival, and the telling of myths and stories.

A BLOSSOMING PEACH TREE frames a contemporary winter house made of saplings and cattail stems much in aboriginal style.

Even though the Kickapoo lived on the prairie and traveled large distances, they did not obtain horses until the 1780's, and even then they did not place a great premium on them. As they moved west, however, and as the whites began to settle Illinois, they quickly adapted to the horse economy and soon built up sizeable herds by raiding the settlers' corrals. In the meantime they walked or used the pirogue that could be readily hollowed out of a tree trunk with the white man's iron tools. By 1816, the Kickapoo living in central Illinois had become completely dependent on horses as they ranged toward the Mississippi River on hunting expeditions. Although they obtained large herds and used the horses as pack animals, the horse did not materially change the culture of the Kickapoo as it had that of the Plains Indians. The Kickapoo continued to live in fixed villages, but the horse provided greater mobility for hunting and raiding.

THE KICKAPOO AND THE FRENCH

The presence of the French traders in the Great Lakes forced the Kickapoo to choose between two alternatives, neither of which would permit them to keep their old ways. If they refused to trade with the Frenchmen, the Kickapoo would be defeated by their old tribal enemies who obtained white man's weapons, but if they did, they would lose their economic self-sufficiency and become dependent upon the fur trade. The Kickapoo hesitated and soon they and

8

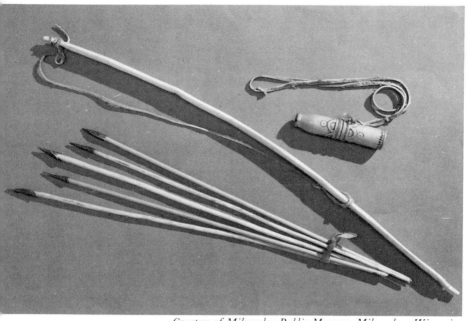

CONTEMPORARY BOW, ARROWS AND DEER CALL made by Kickapoo Indians in Mexico who have preserved traditional craft knowledge and skills.

other Algonquian tribes in Wisconsin experienced pressure from the west by the Sioux with French guns and from the east and south by the Iroquois who were supported by the Dutch and English. These flank tribes had been caught up in the fur trade and they needed more furs and hunting lands to support their new economy. As a result the Kickapoo became the victims along with the other tribes of the bloody trade wars which dislocated many peoples. The Sioux had not been successful in an eastward penetration before, so to avoid annihilation, the Algonquians went to Green Bay and asked for French arms and assistance. The Kickapoo not only received French weapons but in 1685 formed a confederacy with the Mascouten and Fox tribes to repulse the invading Sioux and Iroquois.

The strategy used in fighting was to scatter the villages under war chiefs far enough apart to avoid large defeats, but close enough to give aid. If they chose to take the offensive, they could quickly gather the warriors for a large war party. In one offensive in 1685 they crossed the Mississippi River and successfully fought the Sioux, and then in 1688 they ranged as far east as Niagara in pursuit of the Iroquois.

French traders at Green Bay supplied the usual trade goods of guns, hatchets, knives, and powder flasks, but sought payment from the Kickapoo with pelts. Reliance on this trading economy in turn placed an emphasis on hunting and trapping and reduced the attention to horticulture. As more animals were killed and the hunters sought their game

10

over larger hunting ranges the bands dispersed even more to increase the efficiency of their hunters. This division of the tribe into smaller groups for military as well as economic reasons set the pattern for the next two centuries and still exists today. Migrations that followed in the future years were not conducted by a single large body, but by small groups moving about and settling in different areas. Guns replaced bows, fabrics replaced hides, and iron pots took the place of pottery, and before long the Kickapoo became more and more dependent on French goods.

The Kickapoo, throughout history, were noted because of their resistance to a foreign culture, no matter whose it was. Although they could not stave off economic change, introduced by the French traders, they resisted the religious beliefs of others and refused the education of the white schools. They were especially hostile to French religion, and the mission at Green Bay generally stood empty. In 1680, in Illinois, the Kickapoo killed and mutilated Father Gabriel, a Recollect friar. Not only were these Indians determined to preserve their beliefs, but they harbored a resentment toward the French because of their economic dependence. As a result they frequently attacked French traders and convoys of goods often destined for their enemies the Sioux.

The Kickapoo attacks in the Wisconsin region disrupted trade so extensively that the French were deprived of their profits and the other Indians of the goods they had come to treasure. In the hope of stabilizing the customers, the French convened a

11

gathering of Indians at Montreal in 1701. The Kickapoo, along with the others, attended but, while the others agreed to bury the hatchet, the Kickapoo continued attacking traders and supply trains.

In 1712, Dubuisson, the commandant of Fort Detroit, retaliated by encouraging the Indians friendly to the French to strike back at the Kickapoo confederacy. When some Kickapoo warriors were caught and beheaded and the heads presented at Detroit, the Kickapoo fury exploded into new aggression. The revenge was so severe that the fur trade was further reduced and the French were forced to escalate the war. French troops with Huron, Potawatomi, and Illinois cohorts captured the Kickapoo village on the Fox River and forced the tribesmen to accept peace. The truce was only temporary and soon the Kickapoo were interfering with the French trade again, but on a smaller scale. To avoid another attack some Kickapoo also migrated further south into Illinois where game was more plentiful and where the French presence was not so great. This meant war with the Illinois tribe, however, but that was not distasteful because the Kickapoo remembered the aid that tribe had earlier given the French traders. By 1718, most Kickapoo were living in villages on the Rock River, and the Kickapoo began the first of many steps away from their northern homeland.

The Kickapoo eventually became the friends of the French as the result of an accidental occurrence. In 1728, most of the Kickapoo under Ouiskouba

12

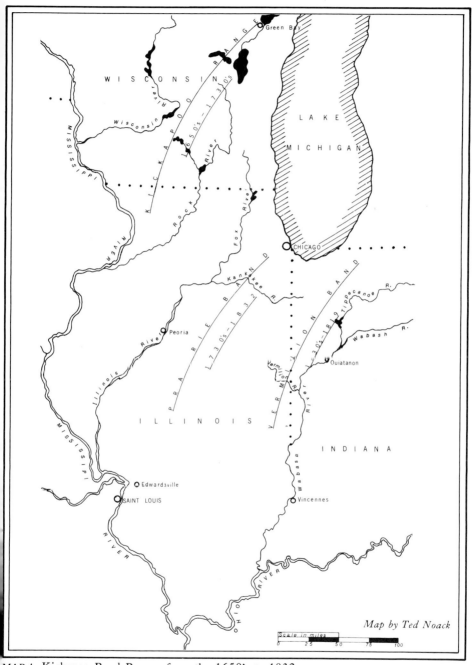

MAP 1. Kickapoo Band Ranges from the 1650's to 1832.

had gone west across the Mississippi River to avoid the French colonials. In this instance the French offensive had been against the Fox, but the Kickapoo feared a similar attack. Shortly thereafter the French traders closed a small post in Sioux territory and the traders under Pierre Boucher traveled down the Mississippi to Illinois country. As the party neared the mouth of the Skunk River, the Kickapoo discovered the traders and forced them ashore. The tribesmen took them captives "for the purpose of saving our children's lives." The Frenchmen were held as hostages. When the Fox learned of the French traders, they threatened and taunted the Kickapoo for not killing the captives, but the Kickapoo realized the necessity of holding live hostages. During the winter the French captives won over the friendship of the Kickapoo, and the constant pressure from the Fox became more and more irritating until the two friendly tribes became enemies.

The Kickapoo, however, had joined a declining power. During this period France fought England in a conflict for empire that would culminate in the French and Indian War and the expulsion of France from North America. Not only did the French colonials use the Kickapoo in expeditions against the Fox, but also to attack the British and their Indian allies.

To insure the loyalty of the Kickapoo, "one of the most turbulent tribes," Beauharnois, Governor of New France, asked them to leave their villages along the Rock River and settle near Ouiatanon, a trading post on the Wabash. They began the migration in

14

1735 and soon the Wabash from Ouiatanon to Terre Haute possessed the major concentration of the tribe. The group that remained for a longer time in that location was known as the Vermillion band after the stream that flows into the Wabash, while the Kickapoo who returned to north-central Illinois near Peoria Lake are called the Prairie band.

The British authorities hoped to break the French trade route to New Orleans. Therefore they armed the Natchez and Chickasaw along the Mississippi River and encouraged them to harass the French expeditions along the river and eventually to carry the attack north of the Ohio River. The Kickapoo were instrumental in turning back the attacks north of the Ohio, and in turn launched extensive and frequent raids against the Chickasaw. So successful were the Kickapoo raiders in the 1740's that the British power was weakened and the French recognized the tribe as a most valuable ally.

British power was too great, however, and by 1759 the French representatives were forced to evacuate the Kickapoo area and retreat to the St. Lawrence River. The British tried to win over the former enemies with gifts of peace, but the Kickapoo did not forgive their old enemy. They readily joined Pontiac, the Ottawa chief, who captured Fort Detroit and hoped to prevent the British occupation of that area. The British peace envoys were unsuccessful, so war with the Indians was the only alternative. After two years of conflict and heavy losses, the British forces broke the rebellion and Pontiac fled westward.

KICKAPOO WINTER CAMP, 1893, still following the pattern of 100 or 200 years earlier, camping at the prairie-forest margin. The lad on the left is holding a lacrosse type stick used

n a game called stick-ball. The horses and wagons are along side the winter houses.

The Kickapoo area was not subdued, however, so the British leaders in 1765 sent a party under the skilled trader George Croghan to again attempt a peaceful solution. As the traders neared the Wabash, they were ambushed by a party of eighty Kickapoo. Several traders were killed and Croghan suffered a hatchet blow to the head — but was saved, in his estimation, by a thick skull. The Kickapoo took the goods, and marched the survivors northward to Ouiatanon where Croghan was held captive by Wahpesah. During his captivity, Croghan, like Boucher, won over the Kickapoo and at the same time was "led a little into the mystery and policy of the people of this country." Croghan also invited the Kickapoo and other tribes to come to councils at Fort Chartres in Illinois and at Detroit. After his release, Croghan met with Pontiac who promised peace with the British colonies. The Kickapoo attended both meetings and agreed to accept the British administration. This did not mean, however, that the Kickapoo would become docile. They raided the English settlements near the forts, stealing livestock and taking captives.

When the Revolutionary War broke out, both British and Americans attempted to win the support of the Indians, including the Kickapoo. Virginia, the state that claimed much of the west, raised an army under the leadership of George Rogers Clark, to drive into the Ohio area in order to protect its property and the Kentucky settlements to the south.

Realizing that his force was too weak to capture Detroit, Clark headed for the forts on the lower Ohio. His strategy was successful and he also won many of the Illinois Kickapoo to his side. They served his army as scouts and kept watch for Chickasaw and Cherokee who threatened to attack from the south.

While the Illinois Kickapoo supported the Americans, the Vermillion band was subjected to British overtures. Henry Hamilton, the British lieutenant governor, invited the Kickapoo to Detroit and showered them with presents. When Hamilton heard that the Virginians were also courting the eastern Kickapoo, he traveled to their villages in December, 1778. With a small war party, the Kickapoo supported Hamilton in recapturing the poorly defended Fort Vincennes and promised to infest the Ohio valley like mosquitoes in spring when the hunt was over. The next February, however, when Clark returned, the Kickapoo chose not to battle their own kinsmen and still remembered their old antagonisms against the British.

The Treaty of Paris of 1783 gave the lands occupied by the Kickapoo to the United States. Clark had explained that the only reason for American presence in the Old Northwest was to defeat the British and promised not to occupy the lands. Even before the Revolution was over, however, American settlers were crossing over from Kentucky. The Kickapoo opposition to the United States grew as the settlements expanded, and the English who refused to evacuate Detroit seemed to be their best hope in reversing American expansion.

THE BATTLE FOR
THE OLD NORTHWEST 1784-1791

Even though the treaty ending the Revolution provided for the removal of British subjects from the land south of the Great Lakes, agents remained and encouraged Indian attacks against the new settlements. The British fur trade would continue to be lucrative if the Indian lands could be retained in the Old Northwest. The Algonquian tribes, including the Kickapoo, needed no urging and struck at the American settlements whenever possible. The Kickapoo concentrated on the lower Wabash and Ohio Rivers, raiding settlements and attacking boats on the rivers. They also made forays into the Kentucky area and returned with plunder.

The governor of Northwest Territory, Arthur St. Clair, hoping to avoid an expensive war, first attempted to maintain peace through an Indian council. He selected Antoine Gamelin, an Indian trader, to bring good-will to the Kickapoo on the Wabash. Instead he received a rebuff and a lesson in Indian diplomacy. A delegation from a respectable government was expected to bring many presents and he had none. The only alternative was a concerted military offensive.

The most successful attack was made in 1791 by General Charles Scott leading Kentucky mounted

20

militia against the Kickapoo village near Tippecanoe Creek. The warriors had heard that an American force had started off for the Miami villages, so the Kickapoo set off to aid their friends, leaving their own villages undefended. When Scott learned that the warriors had gone, he attacked, destroyed the village and its corn, and captured fifty-eight women and children.

Following another attack in that same year by General James Wilkinson when the warriors were west hunting, the Wabash group, with the exception of one band, dispersed. Some went to Missouri, but most went to the Illinois group. The evacuation was not a terrified withdrawal, and the Kickapoo continued with small raids over a period of years. Yet there were also attractions in the West.

THE SPANISH CONNECTION

Back in 1763, at the close of the French and Indian War, France had ceded the trans-Mississippi part of New France to Spain. The first governor, Antonio de Ulloa, decided to strengthen the frontier against England by inviting French traders and Indian tribes into Spanish Louisiana. The friendship of the Kickapoo with the English had been at best lukewarm, so in 1765 one of the bands under Serena accepted the Spanish invitation and built a village on the Missouri River west of St. Louis.

Not all of the Indian tribes in Louisiana were friends of the Spaniards, and the Chickasaw and Osage were especially troublesome. The Chickasaw,

21

for example, continued to attack Spanish expeditions on the Mississippi just as they had attacked French shipping. The Osage, ranging south and west of St. Louis, troubled the Spaniards by ignoring their administration and raiding their settlements.

In 1782, the Spanish governor called on the Kickapoo for help, and they set off immediately to attack the Chickasaw. Learning of the impending Kickapoo attack, the Chickasaw were sufficiently frightened to send Chief Panimataja to St. Louis to sign a treaty which they broke only on occasion. The Spanish officials then had the problem of controlling the Kickapoo, because too much pressure would drive the Chickasaw into the hands of the British traders. Yet Francisco Cruzat, in 1785, admitted that no force could be directed against the Kickapoo because they would retaliate. Only requests for peace would be practical. Against the Osage, the Spanish government recruited the Sac, Fox, and Shawnee, as well as the Kickapoo. Armed with Spanish weapons, these tribes roamed the Osage lands from St. Louis to Natchitoches, taking scalps and selling them to the nearest Spanish buyer. By 1800 the Osage were ready for peace.

When the Spaniards stopped buying scalps and supporting the warriors, many returned to Illinois and Indiana. Serena, however, moved part of his band to the Gasconade River taking over some land previously held by the Osage. Spanish ownership of Louisiana came to an end when Napoleon took it

22

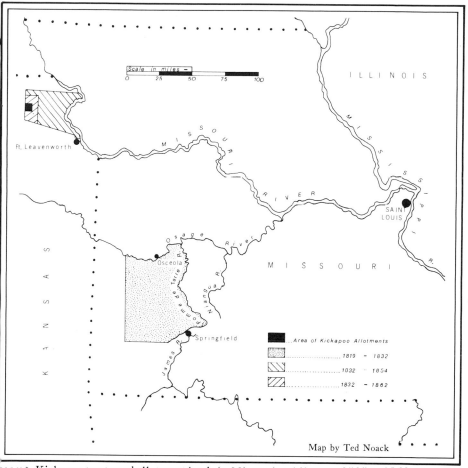

MAP 2. Kickapoo treaty and allotment lands in Missouri and Kansas, 1819 to 1862, showing the progressive loss of tribal lands to the United States government and its citizens.

back, and in 1803, it became part of the United States with the Louisiana Purchase.

THE LAST STAND IN
THE OLD NORTHWEST 1803-1815

When the Kickapoo returned to Illinois and Indiana they found that the Indian resistance had crumbled and the white settlements were advancing rapidly. The new administrator of the area including the Kickapoo range was William Henry Harrison. His purpose was to extinguish Native American title to the land well in advance of settlement so that there would be less inter-ethnic conflict. Harrison was extremely effective in dealing with most of the tribes because they were generally divided on policy. Some tribesmen argued that resistance was futile and that the wise decision was to cooperate with the whites while others called for war. Harrison in 1802 met with the Kickapoo and advised them to turn to agriculture and to give up hunting and raiding. He promised government assistance and held up the Cherokee as an example of a tribe that had made the change. In 1803, at the Treaty of Fort Wayne, he negotiated a land cession on the Wabash near Vincennes by the Kickapoo and other tribes.

Even though the Kickapoo relinquished some land, they could not imagine themselves behind the plow. White settlements came near and incidents between the two races became frequent. The whites insulted and threatened the Kickapoo and the tribesmen stole livestock, burned property, and killed the

25

whites if they resisted. When the British heard of the Kickapoo restlessness, they encouraged them to attend a council at Montreal in 1804. The Kickapoo then began to encourage other tribes to resist the Americans and to attend the British councils. More and more tribes became interested and although there were no overt actions, hostility toward United States citizens grew.

Harrison recognized this alarming trend and tried to counteract it by giving better prices for the furs. He also talked with Pawatomo of the Illinois group and with Oulawau of the Wabash, but nothing was accomplished. Harrison threatened the Indians with destruction by the United States army although he did not relish a war with the Kickapoo whom he considered, next to the Wyandots, the best warriors in the Northwest.

Into this atmosphere of unrest came the catalysts, Tecumseh and his brother Tenskwatawa (The Prophet). They had been living in a Shawnee village in Ohio, but decided that the Kickapoo attitudes and aggressiveness coincided with their views, so they shifted their location to the Wabash. At Tippecanoe Creek, near the Kickapoo village, they built a village for all Indians and called it Prophetstown. Stressing Indian nationalism and hostility to whites, the two leaders attempted to unify the tribes as an effective military barrier to white expansion. Tecumseh preached a return to the old ways, abstinence from whiskey, and holding lands in common so that no one could sell the land to the Americans. By 1811, approximately one thousand people, especially the Kickapoo, had accepted Tecumseh's teachings and had settled near Tippecanoe. British agents from Canada also appeared to lend encouragement and to sell them arms and hatchets.

Tecumseh's eloquence could not heal the division in all of the tribes and there continued to by many who believed that the opposition to the Americans was futile. The Kickapoo also divided on policy, and in 1809 one tribal segment signed a treaty with Harrison yielding three million acres of land west of the Wabash for $800 in goods and an annuity of $400. Tecumseh confronted Harrison near Vincennes and insisted that the land, like the air and sea, belonged to all and could not be ceded.

The British agents encouraged a war against the Americans and there had been enough incidents that no urging was necessary. Tecumseh, in the hope of winning military support from the southern Indians, left with a small bodyguard of Shawnee and Kickapoo Indians. In October and November, 1811, when Tecumseh was still absent, Harrison collected one thousand militiamen to destroy Prophetstown and the neighboring Kickapoo village. Although the Americans lost sixty-one men to approximately thirty for the Indians, Harrison called it a victory. Nine Kickapoo were killed, and the neighboring Kickapoo village was also destroyed.

Instead of subduing the Indians, however, the attack motivated them to respond violently. Not only were they seeking revenge. but they needed food and

27

equipment to replace that which the Americans had destroyed. As the conflict enlarged, even the peaceful tribal factions began turning against the Americans. The warriors were listening more to the urgings of the Prophet than to their own chiefs. Harrison told the Kickapoo to separate themselves from the Prophet and to drive him from the area that did not belong to him. The Prophet eventually left for Canada, but the Kickapoo remained loyal and 160 of the tribe accompanied him to Amherstburg.

The settlers, bearing the brunt of the Indian offensive, retreated from the frontier. Ninian Edwards, Governor of Illinois Territory, petitioned the War Department for some mounted troops for an offensive against the Kickapoo before the foliage became thick enough to conceal their movements. Edwards estimated that there were about 1,500 Indian warriors in Illinois. Among the white population, he could count on only 2,000 persons for militia duty.

There was no immediate assistance from the government, because, in 1812, the United States declared war on England. Tecumseh and the British agents immediately planned several attacks on Northwest posts. The Kickapoo were assigned to take Fort Harrison, a post on the Wabash near Terre Haute. Pakoisheecan planned the attack and arrived at the fort in September. During the night Pakoisheecan pulled himself slowly through the grass by sinking knives into the ground that he held in each hand. He then heaped tinder against the blockhouse wall, set it afire, and hid the flame with his blanket. The warriors then attacked at the opposite side of the fort to distract the defenders from the growing fire. Before the blockhouse collapsed, however, the commander, Zachary Taylor, spotted the potential gap in the defense, and ordered his men to erect a barricade with logs from the headquarters building.

Frustrated, the Kickapoo vented their wrath on civilians. At Pigeon Roost they lifted twenty-one scalps. The army quickly assigned three companies of regulars for Illinois, and Kentucky sent 2,000 mounted riflemen. When the army, under the command of General Samuel Hopkins, reached the middle Wabash, it was discovered by the Kickapoo. The harassment began day and night, and a few days after Hopkins turned west to join forces with Governor Edwards, most of the horses had been frightened away. As the army crossed over sections of dry October grass, the Kickapoo set fires that destroyed much of the equipment, and the Kentuckians returned to the Wabash. There they again attacked the large Kickapoo village near Tippecanoe and destroyed 160 homes.

In the meantime Edwards was more successful against the Illinois Kickapoo. With only 360 men he marched from Edwardsville to Peoria Lake and launched a surprise attack on the village of Chief Pawatomo. This force killed twenty-four Kickapoo, burned the village, and destroyed 1,000 bushels of corn.

The Kickapoo then divided into small bands and scattered well north of the American settlements. At times they penetrated the white patrols and raided settlements. Several hundred Kickapoo crossed the boundary into Canada and joined the Prophet's new village. These Kickapoo participated in the Raisin River Massacre in which over 500 American prisoners-of-war were savagely murdered, and later in October, 1813, they fought in the Battle of the Thames. This battle was an important victory for the Americans, not only because it gave them control of the Northwest, but because Tecumseh was one of the casualties. Most of the tribes accepted defeat and talked peace with Harrison. The Kickapoo, however, remained with the Prophet, at times causing trouble for the Americans, and not until 1819 did all return to the United States.

The British authorities, unable to find victory in the Detroit area, sent Robert Dickson to the Mississippi to probe the strength of the settlements there. Early in 1814 he was at Chief Pawatomo's new village on Rock River distributing presents and arms. Joining forces with the Sac and Fox, the Indians rode south and west against American settlements. The most impressive victory, however, was against a flotilla of barges moving up the Mississippi River to supply the forts upstream. The Indians intercepted the barges near the mouth of the Rock River and killed over 100 Americans.

The war ended in 1815, and with it, British support. The Kickapoo continued their raids, nevertheless, and ignored the appeals for peace of William Clark, Indian Superintendent at St. Louis. The United States convinced the British representative to explain the situation to the Indians, and a meeting was called at Michilimackinac for that purpose. The Kickapoo were told that the Americans did not want their land, only peace, so they met with Clark and Edwards at Portage des Sioux just above St. Louis, in September, 1815. Pawatomo returned to his land near Peoria, and there was peace.

At the end of the war there were about 1,600 Kickapoo including 400 warriors located in Canada, the Vermillion River, central Illinois, and Rock River. Governor Edwards recognized their importance, and in a letter to the Secretary of War suggested that an agent for the tribe be selected with care because, "They are much the bravest and most warlike of all the neighboring savages." They also occupied the strategic position between the settlements and the northern tribes. The Kickapoo could either serve as a barrier to the frontier, or they could become a source of costly depredations.

THE MISSOURI RESIDENCY

The onrush of settlers after the War of 1812 convinced the politicians that more land had to be opened, so in 1816 the United States began negotiations for extinguishing the remaining Indian claims to lands in the Old Northwest and for the removal of the Indians across the Mississippi River. Because of their position near the edge of settlement, the Kicka-

31

poo tried to forestall the white farmers by harassing the surveyors and attacking some new homesteads. Kickapoo proposals to neighboring tribes for unified opposition against the whites were rejected, and the two bands, realizing the futility of further opposition, signed treaties giving up claims to their land east of the Mississippi. At Edwardsville on July 30, 1819, and at Fort Harrison, on August 30, 1819, the Kickapoo gave up their claims to thirteen million acres of land. In return both of the bands received approximately $3,000 worth of equipment, $4,000 annuity for a decade, a tract of land in Missouri, and assistance in the migration.

Reluctantly 1,600 Kickapoo, the majority of the tribe, gathered for the migration in the fall of 1819. Realizing that their frontline defenders were leaving neighboring tribes, such as the Potawatomi tried to forestall their departure by circulating rumors that armed whites were planning violence along the migration route. Although the exodus did take place, the Kickapoo broke into small groups and carefully avoided white settlements. Only 588 of the tribe accompanied Pashal Cerré, the American officer in charge of removal, and that group advanced with great caution.

Some Kickapoo, however, remained on the Wabash until 1823 and 400 people under Mecina and Kennekuk remained in central Illinois until the 1830's. While Kennekuk and his band were peaceful, the warriors of Mecina were not. From their village near Peoria Lake, they rode out stealing horses and destroying property, although they carefully avoided taking lives. The people of Illinois and their elected officials demanded that William Clark, Indian superintendent at St. Louis, remove the Indians, by force if necessary. Clark delayed and sent agents to remind the Kickapoo of the treaty, but he hoped to preserve the good relations he maintained with the Indians under his jurisdiction.

In 1832, Mecina and his followers joined forces with Black Hawk, the Sac leader, who also refused to abide by any treaty that gave up land which held the bones of his ancestors. The United States army and militia drove Black Hawk out of Illinois by force, and the survivors of the 120 Kickapoo who supported him went to Missouri. Kennekuk practiced delay and observed an uneasy peace, remaining until 1834 when he migrated directly to Kansas.

Missouri was not a strange land to the Illinois Kickapoo, because already before the Louisiana Purchase they had served the Spaniards there in the war on the Osage. Other Kickapoo had gone west on winter hunts, and some, such as Serena, remained to establish small villages along the Missouri and Osage Rivers. Lewis and Clark, for example, encountered several of these villages, and one Kickapoo party accompanied the explorers for six days and provided them with fresh meat. More small groups went west during the chaotic period of Tecumseh and the War of 1812. Because they occupied land that was traditionally Osage territory, the Kickapoo were almost in constant conflict with that tribe. In their search for furs and skins, the Kickapoo further antagonized the Osage by ranging south on the Red and Arkansas Rivers, the hunting lands of the Osage. Some of the Kickapoo also raided white settlements in their quest for marketable commodities and took away many horses.

The decision to remove the Kickapoo to Missouri was an unfortunate one because the influx of Kickapoo people simply compounded the problem which the Osage confronted, a scarcity of hunting lands. The white population also was growing, and in 1819, the same year the Illinois treaties were signed, Missouri was populous enough to apply for statehood. The land which the Kickapoo received in Missouri was only sixty miles square, approximately two million acres, and that provided neither enough area for hunting, nor sufficient isolation to avoid inter-ethnic conflict. The Kickapoo also had been under the impression that they were to receive an amount of land in Missouri equal to the area they ceded, and that they would be permitted to select the land they preferred. Instead they discovered that the tract had been assigned to them and that it was smaller than their Illinois range. To show their resentment, they settled east of their tract on the Niangua River. No one, Osage, Kickapoo, or white, was happy with the removal to Missouri.

Superintendent Clark was successful, however, in bringing the Osage and Kickapoo together in 1826 for a treaty of peace. He settled accounts with white settlers who suffered from Kickapoo raids by paying them out of the Kickapoo annuity. As soon as Clark had achieved a peaceful settlement he proposed that the tribe consider yet another step further west and promised them land and agricultural equipment if they would be willing to become farmers. In 1831, Clark heard from his Kickapoo agent that the tribe was willing to examine the land west on the Missouri that Clark had proposed. Although the Kickapoo were not unanimous, the majority favored another migration away from white society and signed the Treaty of Castor Hill in October, 1832, giving up their Missouri lands.

THE KICKAPOO IN KANSAS

The Treaty of Castor Hill provided for a 768,000 acre tract of land in northeastern Kansas and an annuity of $5,000 for nineteen years. Although the Missouri Kickapoo agreed to leave that state, only the 400 followers of Chief Kishko migrated to the new home. The majority turned southward toward Indian Territory and Texas. Kennekuk, the Kickapoo Prophet, however, agreed to leave Illinois, and go west with his 350 people.

There were some basic differences in attitudes between the Kishko and Kennekuk groups and those differences became more pronounced in the Kansas home. Instead of settling in one village, they established two separate villages approximately one mile apart, and while Kennekuk's people turned to agriculture, Kishko's group lived by hunting and trading. During the ensuing thirty years, segment after segment of Kishko's band, including Kishko himself, left to join the Southern Kickapoo until by 1865 only Kennekuk's people remained.

Kennekuk's band profited from the benefits provided in the treaty and accepted farm equipment, livestock, and farm buildings. These Kickapoo also received instruction from the resident agent on farming techniques and soon were producing a surplus of corn, potatoes, cabbage, turnips, and melons which they sold at Fort Leavenworth. They also sold hides and cattle and produced the lumber for their new log cabins.

Although Kennekuk's band quickly adapted to agricultural life, it showed less interest in white man's religion and education. Kennekuk was a mystic who encouraged his followers to live at peace with each other and with the whites. While Kennekuk claimed to possess supernatural powers, he discouraged the observance of old tribal religious practices, including the keeping of the medicine bundles. He became a religious prophet. Some of his ideas and practices were similar to those in white man's denominations, including the prayer board that was used like a rosary. This was simply a board with characters etched in the surface. The worshipper kept track of his prayers by placing a finger on a character. When the Jesuits established a mission among the Kickapoo in 1836, the primary opposition came from Kennekuk who hoped to continue the intellectual domination of his group. The Kishko group, then under the leadership of Pashishi, was more

36

receptive and a few tribesmen attended mass out of curiosity or visited school because of rewards. When Pashishi relocated his village twenty miles away from the mission, the Jesuits abandoned the project. Kennekuk's religion was, nevertheless, a transition between the traditional tribal beliefs and Christianity. In many ways his teaching was beneficial because it discouraged acceptance of white man's vices. Yet it also contributed toward the erosion of older Kickapoo culture by turning away from the traditional beliefs and exposing the Indian mind to Christian beliefs and ethnics, however modified.

The Missouri Kickapoo, who agreed to leave Missouri but did not migrate to Kansas, were entitled to a share of the agreed upon annuity. Each year, therefore, when the annuity was distributed at the Leavenworth Agency, the Kickapoo gathered from all sides to receive their share. This event served to contrast the social and economic development of now separate bands making up the tribe. Eventually most of the Kickapoo migrated southward.

Kennekuk died in 1853 and did not witness the swindle in which the tribe was separated from most of its lands. White settlers, anticipating the creation of Kansas territory, crossed the border from Missouri and squatted on the choice Missouri River lands. Rather than driving off the intruders, the government sent agents to eastern Kansas to purchase land from the various tribes including the Kickapoo. In 1854, the tribe relinquished 618,000 of its 768,000 acres for $300,000, which may seem a princely sum taken together, but which amounts to less than fifty cents per acre.

Even then the problems continued because the remaining land lay astride the transportation routes west, and overland travelers bound for California, Oregon, and Colorado cut Kickapoo timber, stole Kickapoo livestock, and permitted their own cattle to break fences and destroy the crops. Not only did the Kickapoo have choice farming lands, but any enterprising American knew that land along a transportation route was even more desirable. Although the tribe had given up most of its land, it still held 150,000 acres and anyone could see that was too much for only 350 Kickapoo.

The opening wedge for the further United States acquisition of Kickapoo land was a clause in the 1854 treaty that provided for the allotment of a specific tract of land to each family. Owning land in fee simple was not the Indian way and was in direct opposition to their tradition of common ownership. Using threats and misrepresentation, Agent Charles B. Keith was able, however, to make it appear that the tribe approved of allotment. The Kickapoo Allotment Treaty of 1862 called for assignment of 160 acres to each head of family and forty acres, to everyone else. Southern Kickapoo could also receive forty acres, but only the condition that they return to the reserve within one year. Any person who did not wish to receive title to a tract could combine his allotment with others of like mind and could continue to hold the land in common until the govern-

CONTEMPORARY WOODEN SPOONS made by Kickapoo Indians in Mexico, using traditional skills.

ment established a new reservation in Indian Territory. All land not needed for the allotment, approximately 125,000 acres, was declared surplus and sold to the Atchinson and Pike's Peak Railroad for $1.25 per acre.

The resistance to allotment was strong, and over 100 Kickapoo under Chief Nokowhat left in disgust for Indian Territory and Mexico. In doing so, however, they relinquished their claims to the land. By 1869, only ninety-three persons out of 265 who remained had accepted assigned plots. The treaty had also stipulated that under certain conditions the allotments could be sold by the Kickapoo, and many more Indian acres were lost by this process. Those Kickapoo who accepted allotment became citizens of the United States and were the first of their tribe to relinquish their culture.

The transition to another lifestyle was not immediate but by 1879 the agent reported that nearly all of the people were living in non-Indian homes, and that most were wearing textile clothing in the style of other Kansas citizens. They still relied on hunting to supplement their diet and income, but the agent estimated that two-thirds of their subsistence came from farming. Of great importance was the increased attendance at school.

The descendents of the Kansas Kickapoo still live in Brown County and continue their identification as Kickapoo even though many Potawatomi had already entered the tribe in the days of Kennekuk. In 1937, by a vote of thirty-four to twenty-seven they organized themselves as the Kickapoo Tribe of Kansas. This has been of benefit for the group and recently they have been awarded compensation from the Indian Claims commission. In 1945, there were 360 Kickapoo living on 6,399 acres, but there is little social exchange between the Kansas Kickapoo and the Kickapoo of Oklahoma and Mexico. In the years after the Civil War the Southern Kickapoo were in Mexico maintaining their language, their culture, and selecting Kickapoo mates. The Kansas Kickapoo, on the other hand, were becoming more and more assimilated, and that difference broke their unity.

TEXAS AND OKLAHOMA

The first Kickapoo in Texas had been invited as early as 1805 by the Spaniards to settle in the northern and eastern portions of the province. The strategy of the governor, Don Antonio Cordero, was to establish a buffer zone against the encroachments of the neighboring Americans in Louisiana and the raiding parties of the Kiowa and Comanche of the plains. Frequently the Kickapoo mingled with other immigrant Indians such as the Cherokee who had become dissatisfied with white harrassment in the east and with factionalism in their own tribes. One of the major alliances was with Chief Bowles and the Cherokee settlements on the Neches and Angelina Rivers in northeast Texas. There the Kickapoo grazed large herds of livestock, hunted deer and

41

buffalo, trapped fur-bearing animals, and tended fields of corn, beans, and squash.

Another band of Cherokee and Kickapoo, however, under the leadership of Chief Tahchee, established a village along Red River, not far from the future location of Fort Towson, and used it as a base for raids. They robbed any traders in the area, swept eastward to terrorize the new settlements in Louisiana and Arkansas, and rode north to trouble the Osage. In 1828, the Arkansas militia devastated the village and drove the inhabitants southward.

Spain, unfortunately for the Kickapoo, opened Texas to settlers from other nations, and Mexico, when it gained its independence in 1821, continued the program. The majority of settlers came from the United States, and by 1835, the Texas residents wrested their independence from Mexico. At that time Juan N. Almote, a Mexican official, reported 800 Kickapoo in Texas, living primarily north of Nacogdoches.

While the Kickapoo were content with Spanish and Mexican administration, they rejected any overtures from Texas revolutionaries. For a decade both Texas and Mexico appealed to the Indians for support, but the Kickapoo had had their fill of experience with Americans, and never supported Texas. In the early days of the revolution, Sam Houston, Indian Commissioner of the Provisional Government, promised the immigrant Indians continued residence in Texas, although on a more limited range in Cherokee and Smith counties, in return for their neutrality. The Kickapoo did not like the reduction of their land because it revived bitter memories of previous experiences with Americans. The Texas Senate did not approve the concession either, because it wanted the immigrant tribes removed. When Houston became president of the republic, he strove to maintain good will with the Indians and searched for a solution, but that search ended in 1838 with the election of Mirabeau B. Lamar.

Lamar, a resident of Georgia during the time of Cherokee removal, decided to duplicate the program in Texas. Not only were settlers moving northward, but the frontier was in a condition of unrest, partially because of continued agitation by agents of Mexico. The Mexicans, although defeated in the Texas revolution, still hoped to regain the area, or at the very least restrict the growth of the new republic. Vincente Cordova, for example, encouraged the Kickapoo to devastate the frontier and promised the Indians ownership of the Texas lands they occupied.

The Kickapoo, especially those under Benito (Wapanahkah), were receptive to the proposals and led the attack on surveyors and settlers. The Texans under General Thomas J. Rush responded with force and on October 16, 1838, they attacked the Kickapoo Town in northeastern Anderson County that sheltered Benito's warriors and Cordova's Mexicans. During the three-day fight, Cordova fled to Mexico. Eventually one portion of the tribe under Pacana sued for peace and left for Indian Territory, but the others under Benito retreated expecting to fight another day. Some followed Cordova to Mexico.

Pacana settled with his group on the lower Washita and Benito also crossed Red River and built a village further east. As small groups of Kickapoo straggled into Indian Territory, they joined either of the two bands, so that they together soon numbered 1,200. The Kickapoo not only resumed their raids into Texas, but stirred up Indian Territory by raiding the Chickasaw, Choctaw, and Osage, and any white trader who ventured into the border area. The Kickapoo rejected government proposals to join their kinsmen in Kansas, so the army, hoping to reduce the violence and quiet the complaints of the Chickasaw, forced the Kickapoo westward to Wildhorse Creek and began the construction of Fort Washita.

At that time, in 1842, the Creek Nation invited the Kickapoo to settle on the western edge of their land along the Canadian River. The Creek, a peaceful people, asked only that the Kickapoo guard the western and northern border against other marauding Indians, especially the Pawnee. The solution was a satisfactory one, and while the men protected the frontier and hunted, the women planted crops along the Canadian.

Raids against Texas, however, were not abandoned, so some Texas commissioners, hoping to restore peace, invited the Kickapoo to make their homes along the Clear Fork of the Brazos. This location was further west from their original Texas

SEVENTY-FOUR YEAR OLD CHIEF PAPIKWANO, Mexican Kickapoo, 1954, wearing clothing in the style of his generation and standing in front of a summer house.

home, but they had hunted along the Brazos and knew the area abounded in game. About 300 Kickapoo, constituting one-third of the population, left the Creek Nation and followed Mothakuck to Texas. They also found their new home suitable, at least for a while, and lived on venison, turkey, buffalo, and specialized in trading furs and hides. With modern rifles they were successful hunters, and twice a year they brought the furs and hides to Edward's Trading House on the Canadian.

The third group of about 500 people under Benito and Papequah that settled on Wildhorse Creek specialized in trading. Even though they hunted and raised corn and vegetables, they became the middlemen between the trading posts and the Indians of the plains. Each summer they picked up trade items such as tobacco, knives, and cloth from the trading posts and went westward to trade with the feared Comanche. From the Comanche they received horses and mules, generally stolen in Texas and Mexico, as well as captured children. The horses and mules were taken back to the Indian Territory trading houses and sold to buyers from Missouri and Arkansas while the children were generally ransomed at Fort Gibson. Although these three groups were geographically scattered the tribesmen kept in touch and often joined each other in hunts and celebrations.

Even though the Kickapoo found suitable homes and some stability, they were not at peace, especially with their old enemies, the Texans. Not only were the Kickapoo within striking distance of the advanc-

46

ing Texas settlement, but their trade with the Comanche encouraged that large tribe to continue its depredations. When Texas was admitted to the Union in 1845, Indian affairs became the domain of the national government. One federal agent, Robert S. Neighbors, tried setting up trading houses to entice the Comanche away from Kickapoo influence by offering better prices. The Kickapoo spread false rumors about the agent's intentions thereby leading the Comanche to distrust Neighbors' efforts. As a result they continued to be the customers of the Kickapoo and to raid the white settlements for trading materials.

The major problem came when the settlements encroached upon Mothakuck's land on the upper Brazos, and in 1851, he led his people back into Indian Territory. They stopped on Big Beaver Creek which was part of the Leased District and just across the border of Texas. The Leased District was an area north of Red River between the ninety-eighth and one hundredth meridian that the government leased from the Choctaw and Chickasaw for use as a residence for the less civilized tribes of the west. Instead of emulating their eastern neighbors, the Kickapoo teamed up with some Kiowa and Comanche for raids into Texas. They were immensely successful and returned with large horse herds, leaving behind them a wide trail of destroyed property. The army responded by putting more men on patrol, and in 1859, Fort Cobb was constructed on the Washita. Fearing reprisals from the increasing military forces,

KICKAPOO VILLAGE, Mexico, 1954, showing the dispersion of the dwellings and also the

rid nature of the environment.

the Kickapoo left Beaver Creek and joined their relatives on Wildhorse Creek of the Canadian. Quiet settled on the area until the Civil War called the troops to the east and the Kickapoo could move about more freely.

As the Confederates occupied the military posts in Indian Territory, they attempted to enlist the Indians into their armies, or at least obtain promises of neutrality. Most of the tribes complied, but the Kickapoo could not envision the idea of being allied with Texans. In order to avoid reprisals, most of the Southern Kickapoo left Indian Territory for Kansas and either located in southern Kansas or with their kinsmen near Fort Leavenworth. Those in southern Kansas lived on the Walnut and Neosho Rivers, but raided south into Indian Territory and returned with cattle and horses for sale to the Union army contractors. Eventually some Kickapoo became discontented in their dealings with Union officials and their proximity with the Osage Indians and left for Mexico.

MEXICO

The first Kickapoo to migrate to Mexico had done so in 1838 when the Texas army dislodged the Mexican-Indian forces in northeast Texas. The Mexican government had settled the fugitives along the Rio Grande near Morelos and employed them as frontier defenders guarding against Apache and

Comanche raids. The Mexican Kickapoo also retained their hatred for Texas and periodically raided across the Rio Grande.

The second experience of the Kickapoo with Mexico came in 1850 when Wildcat, a Seminole warrior, tried to establish an Indian colony in Mexico, beyond the reach of the United States. Most of the tribes, upon hearing the proposals of Wildcat, displayed no interest, but the Kickapoo remembered the white harassment and a party under Papequah agreed to migrate. The Mexican officials also welcomed the Seminole-Kickapoo band and promised them land, livestock, and agricultural tools if they would bolster the forces along the Rio Grande. Even though they were successful in their battles with the Comanche and Apache, the Wildcat followers listened to the entreaties of chiefs Pacanah and Pecan, who had journeyed to Mexico all the way from Indian Territory, and accompanied them back to the United States.

As a result of the dislocation of the Civil War and the problem of neutrality, 600 of the Southern Kickapoo under Machemanet, successor of Mothakuck, left southern Kansas for Mexico at the close of 1862. The Mexican government welcomed them and provided land near Nacimiento, on the frontier, with the same duties as before. Those Kickapoo who remained in Kansas soon changed their mind when the Union armies conquered Indian Territory and discouraged further Kickapoo raids.

By 1865, all of the Southern Kickapoo had accepted the invitation of the Mexican government and had crossed the border.

Most of the migrating bands encountered no difficulty crossing Texas by traveling west of the one hundredth meridian, but in January, 1865, one of the largest parties led by Pecan, Papequah, and Nokowhat of the Northern Kickapoo, was forced to fight. The group had traveled slowly across the Texas Panhandle hunting buffalo as it went. Although aware of possible attack from the Texans, the Kickapoo did not know that their trail had been spotted by a Texas scouting patrol. The Confederate Army at Fort Chadbourne and the militia of the area were alerted and began pursuit. In the meantime the Kickapoo had made camp behind a bluff on Dove Creek, approximately sixteen miles south of the present city of San Angelo, waiting out a snow storm. Confident that no one would be looking for Indians in such bad weather, no guards were posted. On the morning of January 8, however, the Texas force of 400 attacked and easily captured the horses. Sufficiently warned by the preliminary thrust, the Kickapoo in the camp quickly grabbed their Enfield rifles and took cover. They returned the fire and followed with a fierce counterattack that regained their horses and drove the Texans to retreat. Not realizing that there would be no renewed attack, the chiefs ordered the evacuation of the camp and rushed for the border taking only the barest necessities. The Texans lost twenty-six men, and sixty others were

52

critically wounded. So shameful was the defeat that an official investigation was ordered.

The Mexican Kickapoo welcomed this large group into their homes while the Mexican officials, eager to add them to the defense lines, provided more land and agricultural supplies. The Kickapoo, then numbering approximately 1,300 attempted to provide for themselves through agriculture, hunting, and collecting bounties on Comanche and Apache scalps. After Appomattox, however, the Union armies were sent west to pacify the Indians of the frontier, and the Comanche and Apache raids were significantly curtailed. To compensate for their loss of income, the Kickapoo initiated a campaign of raids into Texas that grew easily out of their long-standing hatred of the Texans.

Taking advantage of the protection granted by the international boundary, the Kickapoo raiders crossed the Rio Grande in groups of thirty to fifty well-mounted, well-armed warriors. They ranged as far south as Laredo, as far north as Terrell County, and as far east as San Antonio. In their lightning attacks, lasting only three to four days, they collected horses and cattle, kidnapped women and children, stampeded flocks of sheep, and killed any Texan who resisted. Driving the livestock across the Rio Grande, the Kickapoo sold them to the Mexican merchants who retailed them in turn for a handsome profit. The local politicians approved and cooperated by supplying papers and documents indicating Kickapoo ownership of the livestock. Texas ranchers who crossed the border to regain their property were prevented from doing so by canny local officials on the ground that the animals were spoils of war.

Protection against these raiders was difficult not only because it was impossible to anticipate their movements, but also because they moved so rapidly. By frequently changing mounts they covered many miles of the sparsely populated ranch land and when pressed they could always take refuge behind the border. Posses or military companies who made contact with the Kickapoo were confronted with excellent fighters, and never was an entire party of raiders ever eliminated. This period of time was also the era of Reconstruction in Texas when an impoverished state tried to re-establish itself and had problems enough controlling its own civilian population.

Finally in 1872, Congress, answering petitions and appeals authorized an investigation. In their final report the commissioners estimated that 14,000 horses and 500,000 cattle had been stolen between 1865 and 1872. The Bureau of Indian Affairs, believing the best solution was to return the Kickapoo to a location in Indian Territory, asked Agent Jonathan B. Miles to advance the idea to the Mexican group. Accompanied by some Kansas Kickapoo leaders, Miles found that many, especially the women, were willing to return, but most of the men, listening to the local Mexicans, preferred to stay. The Coahuila officials also countered Miles's overtures with $5,000 worth of gifts, fully realizing that Kickapoo removal would open their area for

Apache raids and that they would lose the trade of Texas cattle and horses. The Miles proposals were rejected and the raids into Texas continued. Other attempts at a diplomatic solution with Mexico also proved fruitless, so the United States Army prepared to solve the problem in its own way.

Colonel Ranald S. Mackenzie was told by General Philip Sheridan to "clean up this situation" with his Fourth Cavalry. This order implied disregarding Mexican sovereignty by crossing the border without permission. The United States earlier had requested approval for the cavalry to cross when in hot pursuit of the Kickapoo, but the request had been denied. Sheridan assured Mackenzie of full support from senior officers.

Mackenzie prepared his men at Fort Clark approximately fifty miles north of Eagle Pass, with rigorous drill and careful inspection and maintenance of all equipment and gear. With equal attention he interviewed residents of the area and sketched rough maps showing trails and fords across the river. Mackenzie further enlisted the assistance of some Negroes living near the Kickapoo villages whose ancestors had been former slaves of the Creeks and Seminoles. These people, called Muscogees, long resented the arrogance of their Kickapoo neighbors and happily accepted Mackenzie's offer that they act as spies. During the night of May 16, 1872 a messenger rode into Mackenzie's headquarters with the announcement that the Kickapoo warriors had gone west for a hunt. Mackenzie broke camp that morning and led

55

his force to the Rio Grande. That night the Fourth Cavalry crossed into Mexico near El Moral and, following the back trails, covered the seventy miles to the Kickapoo village by dawn. After a brief rest they moved closer to the village and suddenly attacked. Not prepared, the Indians fought as best they could, but soon fled while the troops set fire to the lodges. Nineteen Kickapoo were killed and the forty women and children who were captured were mounted on ponies and rushed to the border. Still fearing pursuit by the Kickapoo, Mackenzie pushed on with the exhausted and hungry prisoners until they reached San Antonio. From there they were taken to Fort Gibson and held as prisoners of war by the War Department.

In the meantime, the representatives of the Bureau of Indian Affairs, led by Henry M. Atkinson, arrived in Saltillo completely unaware of the Army's radical action. In Saltillo the commissioners received permission from the governor of Coahuila to conduct another session with the Kickapoo on the subject of a peaceful removal. The Kickapoo survivors had scattered after the raid, fearing other reprisals, but when they heard that food and clothing was available in Santa Rosa, they slowly drifted in. Most of the Indians who came to the commissioners were relatives of the captives and deeply concerned for their welfare. The Kickapoo expressed no new desire or intention of migrating to Indian Territory, and the commissioners soon realized that removal would be accomplished only by insisting that a re-

Courtesy of Oklahoma Historical Society

SUMMER HOUSE OF THAH PE QUE, head chief of the Kickapoo. The photograph was made in Oklahoma after the return of the Kickapoo from Mexico in 1874. The ox yoke and two plows illustrate the attempts at commercial agriculture.

union with the captives take place in Indian Territory. After the commissioners gave assurances of protection and when $8,000 worth of food and equipment was distributed, 317 persons including chiefs Chequamkako and Thahpequah agreed to travel to the United States. The party, accompanied by Atkinson, arrived at Fort Sill in December, 1873, and set up temporary quarters on the Washita.

In 1875, Atkinson again returned to Mexico hoping to convince the remaining Kickapoo to move to Indian Territory. The Kickapoo, living in fear of another raid, had remained scattered, so Atkinson went to Santa Rosa, sent out word of his presence, and waited. Some bands drifted in to talk, but Atkinson's efforts were off-set by Mexican citizens who still feared Apache raids and who also realized the economic advantages of retaining the remaining tribesmen. By April, Atkinson had convinced only 115 Kickapoo under Mosquito to migrate, and in October thirty more followed.

The Kickapoo who were determined to remain in Mexico returned to their raids of Texas in 1876, stealing horses and cattle and killing citizens. By then there were fewer Indians and more troops, and whenever an Indian camp was located the cavalry crossed the boundary, destroyed it, and killed the occupants. Exhausted and decimated by 1880, the Kickapoo reluctantly gave up their war with Texas and became agricultural.

In recent times the Mexican Kickapoo, numbering approximately 387, live on a reservation of

17,000 acres. The village, one mile square in size, is called El Nacimiento Ranchería and is located within twenty-five miles of the Mexican town of Musquiz. The inhabitants engage in subsistence agriculture and grazing, with periodic deer hunts. The area is vulnerable to droughts, however, so that agriculture is small scale subsistence at best. Hunting also has become more difficult as ranchers have built fences and often object to hunters, but characteristically the Indians insist that the deer do not belong to the ranchers because they carry no brands. Buckskin, moccasins, and baskets provide only a small source of income.

Nevertheless, the Mexican Kickapoo have maintained many of their Algonquian customs, such as the style of housing. They still construct the wickiup in the old way, but in Mexico they use rush mats exclusively for covering the buildings instead of birch bark and cattail mats. The dry, hot climate of Mexico has forced the abandonment of other implements, but deer calls, cradleboards, moccasins, wooden ladles, and mortars and pestles are used as they were in the Wisconsin days. Much of the diet remains as it was in Wisconsin because deer hunting is possible in Mexico and corn can be grown with irrigation. The Kickapoo have accepted the Mexican sombrero, the donkey and currency, but the Spanish language has not replaced the native language. Some Kickapoo, especially the women, speak no Spanish whatever.

The part of the culture most resistant to change is

the religious life. Other religions have been rigorously excluded, not only the Catholic Church, but also the peyote religion. There are four sacred bundle societies whose primary ceremonies take place in February in conjunction with the celebration of the New Year's ceremony. Here the bundles of deerskin containing pipes, flutes, and beads are opened and renewed. The traditional costumes including buckskin moccasins, loincloth, and leggings, as well as long-sleeved cotton shirt, are worn only at these celebrations. The usual clothing worn at work is the same as that of the neighboring Mexican. Religious practices are closely guarded by the tribe and whites are excluded from the performances of religious ceremonies. The social and political structure of the tribe also remain largely unchanged.

The Kickapoo from the two communities in the United States and Mexico visit back and forth, and sometimes there is a marriage between them. The Mexican Kickapoo community is the more traditional of the two because it is more isolated geographically and the Mexican government has been more tolerant. When the Mexican government, however, tried to introduce new ways through public education, the Kickapoo resisted and burned the school buildings. In recent years the Mexican Kickapoo have participated in migratory labor in the United States and as a result have been exposed to a different culture. Isolation has become difficult for the Kickapoo community and attrition of the old ways will be more accelerated.

PEHKOTAH, born in 1851, residing in Mexico in 1907 after migrating from Oklahoma under Martin J. Bentley's direction. From photograph by DeLancy Gill.

While the Kickapoo had been away in Mexico, the United States punished the Five Civilized Tribes because of their affiliation with the Confederate States of America by taking away much of their land. Smaller tribes from all over the country, but especially Kansas, were then settled on the unoccupied area. The Kickapoo were late-comers, and by 1874, the choice of unassigned land was limited.

The Indian agent, Andrew Williams, selected a tract in the northern part of the territory, just west of the Osage reservation. When the Kickapoo arrived from Mexico, they refused to accept the location, primarily because of its proximity to the Osage, and insisted that they select the reservation as Atkinson had promised them. The Kickapoo therefore wintered on the upper Washita, subsisting off government supplies and looking forward to the spring when they would select their own land.

The old home site on the Canadian had been assigned to the Shawnee, but there was vacant land nearby, just west of the Sac and Fox. The Kickapoo language was similar to that of these two tribes, and the land between the Deep Fork and the North Fork of the Canadian was fertile and well-watered. The choice was made. The Kickapoo built a village of traditional houses and planted fields of corn, squash, beans, and pumpkins. They hunted on land to the west, sold the skins, and existed without government aid for a while. Instead of setting up a new agency, the Bureau of Indian Affairs placed them under the jurisdiction of the Sac and Fox Agency.

This happy beginning was marred by complaints from the other tribes such as the Chickasaw, Kiowa, and Wichita, who objected to the effective hunting of the Kickapoo on their lands. They also charged the Kickapoo with stealing their horses. The immediate neighbors, the Sac and Fox, and the Shawnee were not as resentful, and joined the Kickapoo in their religious observances, games, and festivals. This behavior distressed the white reformers who observed not only strong resistance to civilization from the Kickapoo but the backsliding in other tribes as a result of Kickapoo encouragement. Agricultural work was left to the women and the men gambled, raced horses, and played cards. Instead of being grateful that the Kickapoo had abandoned their marauding ways, the Indian officials decided to break down Indian culture with white education. While education had been readily accepted by many tribes, the Kickapoo viewed the school as an offense to the Great Spirit and something to be resisted. The building erected for educational purposes remained vacant until 1876, and then it was used for the storage of horse feed.

The Kickapoo were more receptive toward the ways of the white farmer and began to raise cattle, hogs, chickens, and use farming equipment. The Bureau of Indian Affairs provided the services of a station farmer to give advice and instructions in agricultural methodology. The Kickapoo were not willing to accept allotment, however, and bitterly rejected the idea each time it was proposed. When Agent John Pickering proposed the idea and hinted that rations could be withheld until they accepted it, the Kickapoo responded by threatening to return to Mexico. Pickering yielded but failed to understand why the tribe was so determined to avoid civilization and to stay with Indian ways. He should have remembered the advice given him in 1875 by Atkinson on the best way of handling Mosquito's band: "They can be led, but not driven."

The resourceful Kickapoo also employed some Mexicans, Creeks, and Negroes to do their field work with money gained by other methods. They often roamed off on hunting expeditions or stole cattle from the Texas herds bound for the Kansas cow towns. The skins not needed for their own use were sold, while the cattle were driven to the Unassigned Lands in the center of the Territory and traded off to white renegades for whiskey and ammunition. The Kickapoo continued to live in bark lodges, to boycott schools, and to celebrate their religious festivals. In 1886, after living on their reservation for ten years, they cultivated only 175 acres, and in 1890, the total was only about 300 acres. In the meantime, the United States spent over $100,000 on equipment and rations. In addition to farming equipment the government provided rations of beef, flour, sugar, coffee, soda, salt, and tobacco; medicine such as liniment and eye salve; and other items including

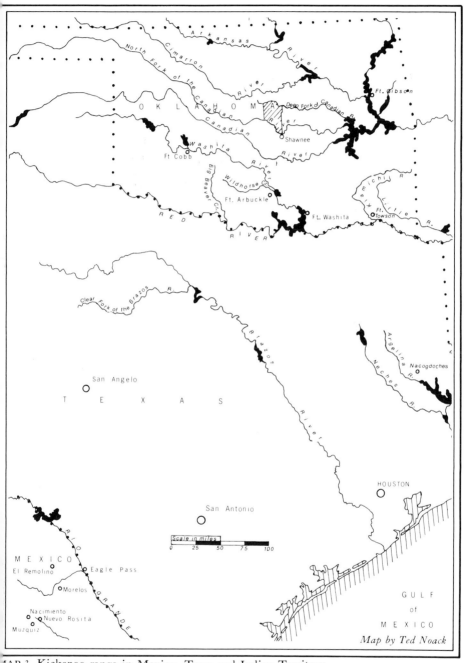

MAP 3. Kickapoo range in Mexico, Texas and Indian Territory.

thimbles, ear bobs, fish lines, and perfumery. The Kickapoo had no intention of giving up these gifts and continued to demand and receive them during the entire reservation period.

The greatest agony for the Kickapoo came in 1899 when the Unassigned Lands, a track bordering the reservation on the west, was opened for settlement. In the long run, this decision began the white occupation of Indian Territory that would eventually over-run most of the Kickapoo land, and in the short run, it brought in neighbors who had no respect for Kickapoo timber and grassland. When the agency requested troops to protect tribal lands, no help came, but when the Kickapoo decided to protect their lands themselves, the army arrived and confiscated the warriors' weapons. The white neighbors included farmers interested in land, as well as liquor peddlers, confidence men, and gamblers interested in anyone with wealth. They helped break the boredom of reservation life, but they also separated the Kickapoo from what little money they had.

While the white presence in the new district can be considered as the most successful instrument in the destruction of Kickapoo culture, a second element was the influence of a group of approximately forty Kickapoo from Kansas who, in 1878, joined their kinsmen in Indian Territory. Under the leadership of Keoquark, these Kansas Kickapoo were more comfortable with white civilization and most were capable of making a significant adjustment to white culture. They became the core of the Progressive

66

Kickapoo who preferred eliminating tribal control and accepting allotment. The tribe was therefore split between the "Progressive" and the "Kicking Kickapoo" or the "Kickers." The Progressives appealed to the young and the faction grew in members, so that by 1890, the year after the opening of the Unassigned Lands, over 100 out of the population of 400 subscribed to their philosophy.

The Progressives opened the door for white ideas when in 1890 they invited Elizabeth Test, a Quaker, to begin the instruction of their children. All of the earlier attempts had ended in failure, even though the government and the Society of Friends had valiantly tried to keep the schools open. Elizabeth Test had arrived on the reservation in 1885, but the school she opened was never attended. During that time she remained on the reservation and gradually won over some people with her kindness. After a while, however, her health broke, and she went to work in the more congenial atmosphere of the Iowa Tribe. When she returned to the reservation, she opened school in a tent with nine pupils. As more children came, she built a permanent school near McLoud with her own savings. In 1892, she became the Kickapoo Field Matron for the tribe and received a government salary. Unfortunately for the Kickapoo, gradual acquaintance with white culture was not achieved. In 1895 when the reservation was broken up, the tribesmen were thrown out into a white society with which they were poorly equipped to deal.

The opening of the Unassigned Lands created no specific problem of jurisdiction because no Indian tribe had claim to the area. Other parts of the territory, however, though sparsely populated, were specifically granted to various tribes. If more land were to be made available to whites, the consent of the tribes would be necessary. The Dawes Act, passed in 1887 as reform legislation, provided the solution. Under this act, Indians could break up the reservation, receive allotments of land, and then live like white farmers. One tribe after another accepted allotment of lands and sold off the land left over to white settlers.

The Sac and Fox lands were opened in 1891, and the pressure on the Kickapoo to do the same with their more fertile acres became intense. A three-man commission, known generally as the Cherokee Commission, spoke with the various tribes, including the Kickapoo, about accepting allotment. Every visit by the commission was resisted by the Kickapoo because the tribe considered the ownership of land in common to be a religious mandate.

At this point a conspiracy was hatched to force the allotment of Kickapoo lands, John T. Hill, a former United States deputy marshall, notified the tribe that there was some money in Washington, D. C. and that he was willing to help them obtain it. The tribe empowered Hill, an interpreter, Joe Whipple, and

68

two chiefs, Ockquanocasey and Keeschocum, to go to Washington and get the money, but also to ensure the tribal ownership of their lands. Through deceit and threats a document was signed that was in actuality an agreement to allotment.

Two years later in 1893, Moses Neal, special agent, arrived on the reservation to begin the allotment selection. The Kickapoo refused to be enrolled and sent Papashekit, who knew some English, to Washington. Ignored by officials he finally went to the Indian Rights Association and convinced them of the need for an investigation. The Association concluded that the entire procedure had been fraudulent, but the House Committee on Indian Affairs, aware of the objections, recommended that Congress approve the Kickapoo Allotment Bill.

The United States deprived the Kickapoo tribe of its 206,000 acres for $64,650. While it distributed $4,478 among the tribesmen, the United States paid $5,172 to John T. Hill, and retained $5,500 in the United States Treasury at five per cent interest. The Kickapoo received slightly more than thirty cents per acre while other tribes received $1.50. Instead of receiving allotments of 160 acres, the Kickapoo received only eighty acres. Even though the Kickapoo allotment law passed Congress in 1893, Kickapoo resistance and the refusal to be enrolled prolonged the allotment process for two years.

Of the 206,000 reservation acres, 87,000 was granted to Oklahoma as school land and the remaining 101,000 was opened for the last of the exciting land runs. Thereafter the General Land Office used the more peaceful lottery system.

Instead of accepting their allotments as the "Progressives" did, the conservative "Kickers" under Wahpahhoko occupied the 87,000 acres granted for schools. Many lawyers offered their services to the Kickapoo for redress of grievances resulting from the inequitable allotment act, but the "Kickers" hired Martin J. Bentley to advise them. Bentley lived with the Kickapoo, and eventually the Bureau of Indian Affairs, on the request of the "Kickers," appointed him special agent for the group. He defended them in liquor-related cases, free of charge, and protected the Kickapoo as well as he could from the greed of the whites. Of all the agents, Bentley was the most popular because, in addition to defending them, he did not insist on their giving up the old ways. He countenanced their horse racing, poor school attendance, and frequent dances and celebrations. He even told them that if they moved to their allotments, he would look for a place where they once more could hold land in common and live by hunting. The land he had in mind was in Mexico and he personally traveled to that country to make arrangements. At least he peacefully removed the Kickapoo from the school lands and settled them on the allotments.

After six years of service, in 1901, Bentley was retired from his position as special agent and replaced by Frank Thackery. The removal was not arbitrary action by the Commissioner of Indian Affairs, because he had heard of Bentley's Mexican ventures

70

Courtesy of Smithsonian Institution, National Anthropological Archives
WAH PE CAT QUA, head chief of the Kickapoo from 1901-1908.
From a print by Martin J. Bentley.

and directed him to abandon the scheme and perform the duties assigned to him. The removal was a disappointment for the tribe because the people had been pleased with Bentley's tolerant administration. It was also a disappointment for Bentley because it damaged his plans. Not only was he planning to remove the Kickapoo to Mexico, but he expected to receive in return the 18,000 acres the Kickapoo still owned.

The 1893 law that provided for the allotments awarded the Indians the patents of ownership, but prohibited the transfer of title for twenty-five years. The land could be leased, however, and if the owner died, the land could be sold by the survivors. Bentley moved to the town of Shawnee where he practiced law and continued to serve the Kickapoo clients especially in leasing or disposing of heirship lands. Kickapoo reliance on Bentley was an irritation to Thackery, and Thackery soon began to suspect Bentley's honesty. Thackery also discovered that Bentley had convinced the Kickapoo to place money from the leases and sales of lands into a tribal treasury that would eventually be used to relocate the tribe in Mexico. In the meantime, Bentley transported equipment and tribesmen, especially young heirs, to Mexico. This procedure enabled him to sell the wards' lands and charge his commission without interference.

The first opportunity for big profits came in 1905 when Congress issued patents in fee to seven owners of allotments on the outskirts of Shawnee, Oklahoma. Bentley obtained the warranty deeds for each of the allotments and sent the former owners to Mexico. He in turn sold the tracts at a sizeable profit. By 1905, Bentley had arranged the migration of over 200 Kickapoo to Mexico and only about 100, nearly all Progressives, remained on the allotments.

Because of Thackery's complaints, the Bureau of Indian Affairs sent an inspector, Charles Dickson, to Oklahoma and to Mexico to study the problem. Dickson's findings substantiated Thackery's charges. When he traveled to Mexico he found the newly arrived tribesmen in a temporary camp near Musquiz — many suffering from malnutrition and poverty. The Mexican Kickapoo were not happy to see their kinsmen who had become tainted with white ways, and neither was the Mexican government.

Unfortunately, Congress ignored the Dickson report and in 1906 passed a law removing the restrictions on the sale of all allotments held by non-resident adult members of the tribe. This law enabled Kickapoo landowners in Mexico to sell their land before the trust period expired, but it also encouraged the Oklahoma residents to leave for Mexico in order to sell their land. With the passage of the law, land-hungry whites descended on Musquiz looking for landowners who could be induced to sell. Bentley had already arrived and laid plans to get the land himself. He talked to the Kickapoo warning them of the land buyers and he also purchased the cooperation of Alberto Guajardo, the Mexican official at Musquiz. The Shawnee, Oklahoma, land buyers evidently paid Guajardo more than Bentley did, because suddenly Bentley was in jail. The Kickapoo were herded to Eagle Pass, Texas, where they signed deeds before Texas notaries. Those who hesitated were threatened, beaten, and jailed. Many of the documents were forged.

After the Shawnee land buyers had left with their freshly signed papers, Bentley got out of jail and turned to help the demoralized tribesmen. He moved them westward to northern Sonora, twenty miles south of Douglas, Arizona, and settled them on an abandoned ranch. He then returned to the United States and cooperated in the exposure of the land purchasers. The Senate subcommittee investigated the scandal and concluded that the Shawnee land buyers had committed crimes. A special attorney was employed to investigate the titles and recover the lands for the Kickapoo. Questions were also raised about Bentley's role in the affair, but he was vindicated and no attempts were made to recover the land he had obtained.

Agent Thackery had been involved in the case as well, but he had not been satisfied with the exoneration of Bentley. As a result of painstaking research, he charged Senators Henry Teller and Charles Curtis of collusion with Bentley. Because of the efforts of Thackery and John Embry, United States attorney, the courts in 1911 directed that the land be returned to the Kickapoo claimants. The appeals postponed final settlement until 1914.

KICKAPOO INDIANS migrating to Mexico, 1907. From a print by Martin J. Bentley.

Return of the lands was never an adequate compensation for the financial loss suffered during this twenty-year period, much less for the emotional strain and mental anguish. There was no way that the Mexican Kickapoo could be convinced that the supervision of the Indians would remain benevolent, so once again they were lured back to Oklahoma. Some returned in 1916, but the majority wandered between Bacerac, the colony in desert-like Sonora, Nacimiento, and Oklahoma. More and more Mexican Kickapoo settled along the Canadian River over the next decade, but not until the 1920's did the Kickapoo return in significant numbers.

THE KICKAPOO IN
CONTEMPORARY TIMES

Following the allotment of their lands, the Kickapoo lost government rations and direct assistance, and were forced to make the transition to an agricultural society. The Bureau of Indian Affairs continued to supervise the leasing of lands and to provide agricultural advisors, but the ultimate goal was assimilation into white economic life. Although raising food for themselves was part of their experience, the Kickapoo found the adjustment to commercial farming difficult. Even so, many turned to cotton farming with moderate success until the boll weevil destroyed productivity. They lived in general at a subsistence level and became another element of the rural poor.

During the 1920's and 1930's the Oklahoma

76

Kickapoo continued to seek isolation from white civilization by building their homes away from roads. As time passed, however, more constructed small frame houses next to their traditional wickiups and lived in both. Their usual attire became cotton clothing and work clothes in the style of the rural whites, although the traditional clothing was worn at festivals. The food, however, was less like that of the whites because it included more corn, beans, and squash. The corn, prepared in the traditional way, was crushed with wooden mortar and pestle and then boiled. Fry bread, made of wheat flour, salt, and baking soda, and fried in deep fat, was also popular.

In November, 1930, a subcommittee of the Senate conducted hearings in Shawnee on the conditions of the Indians on the agency. Because the Kickapoo such as George Kishketon, Wah-Pe-Pah, Ah Kahtu Sheme, and Sweeney Stevens were asked to bring their problems to the subcommittee, these reports provide a valuable glimpse into Kickapoo life between the land controversy and World War II.

The Kickapoo had given up the fight against white schools and all of the children between the ages of six and eighteen were either enrolled in school or physically unable to attend. The parents, however, were financially unable to properly clothe the children and to provide them with lunches if they attended local public schools. The Kickapoo hoped that the government would assist their children just as it did those youngsters who attended boarding schools, so that the parents could keep them in the family and yet reduce the distinction between white and Indian children at the school.

Medical facilities were inadequate because there was no general hospital in the vicinity. A tuberculosis sanitarium was nearby, but its 100 beds were taken and the Kickapoo suffered from other illnesses as well. Trachoma and pellagra were major health problems and most sicknesses reported in the tribe were related to dietary deficiencies and inadequate cleanliness. The Kickapoo not only needed a hospital, but hoped their men could get jobs on the anticipated construction project.

Land ownership and land sales continued to be a matter of concern even after all the attention to it twenty years earlier. The Kickapoo were worried about the possibility of county taxation of their land. Under the 1906 law nonresidents could sell inherited land, but if some of the heirs sold and others did not, would the land be taxed? What happened if the Kickapoo sold land and was not a resident? What made a person a nonresident? Not only would the Kickapoo be unable to pay tax, but understandably any business dealing, which threatened to involve the Kickapoo with government, was psychologically unnerving. A. W. Leech, Superintendent of the Shawnee Agency believed that the taxation issue was raised so that the Kickapoo would worry and be more ready to sell his holding. Leech specifically named Charles Dashane, a former clerk at the Shawnee Office, and others, who were trying to buy Kickapoo land at cheap prices. The national government

78

should have repealed the 1906 law or at least re-assured the Kickapoo that they would not be taxed.

The Kickapoo were completely dissatisfied with the government farmer, Charles Edmister. They considered him lazy and presented a list of grievances against him. One of the tasks of the farmer was to assist the Kickapoo in planning and supervising the construction of a house or building. Kishketon cited several examples of how Edmister's costs were too high and that he was providing business for a relative who was a builder. The complaints against Edmister were minor ones, or the results of misunderstanding, but he was the white man who most frequently became involved in the day-to-day life of the Kicka-poo. They wanted him available whenever they needed him and in that sense his independence was like that fastener on the agency door. They hoped it would be removed so they could have free access to the agency.

While the Kickapoo and other Native Americans drifted through the post-allotment period, the policy makers belatedly realized the mistake of that program. The Wheeler-Howard Act of 1934 authorized most tribes of the United States to re-establish tribal government while the Thomas-Rogers Oklahoma Indian Welfare Act of 1936 included the Kickapoo. Although the laws enabled the Native Americans to establish political organizations for their tribes, nothing was done by the Kickapoo about gathering the lands they still held into a single reservation. The damage done by the allotment program

WINTER LODGES on the property of Joe Murdock, 1927, stand in contrast to white man's

wagons, telephone line, and frame building used primarily for cooking.

was therefore not reversed, and the Kickapoo never regained their land base. As a result the Kickapoo are scattered on holdings that remain on the north bank of the North Canadian River from Jones to Shawnee, and maintain their unity only through being members of the Kickapoo Tribe of Oklahoma.

Tribal membership is available for all persons who possess one-fourth or more Kickapoo blood and are not enrolled with another tribe. Although there are 1,184 members on the tribal roll, only about 500 live in the original reservation area. The trust land which the individuals hold is not taxed, but since the days of the original small allotments the land that was not sold has been willed through several generations. As a result very few Kickapoo farm their own lands because many heirs own rights to the same allotment. Most lands are leased and the rent divided into small portions. In early 1975, 6,128 acres remained with Kickapoo owners. In 1950 they had held 8,817 acres, so Kickapoo lands continue to fall into alien hands.

The tribal government, established in 1937, is administered by a Business Committee which is composed of five persons: the elected officers of the tribe and one councilman. The powers assigned to the tribal government are limited to transacting business for the tribe. The Kickapoo, however, have no reservation to administer, no court for their own people, nor do they supervise a tribal enterprise. At the time when the organization first came into being,

Courtesy of Oklahoma Historical Society

OSCAR WILDE, *Ka-kan-dji-ga*, 1926, in his medicine costume.

the meetings were informal and infrequent. Little business was proposed for consideration, and the meetings were held in the chairman's home or in the tribal meeting house. There was no tribal budget, and funds for the operation of the office were raised by holding pie suppers and box socials. In recent years the tribe received land from the Society of Friends and presently owns seventeen and one-half acres two miles north of McLoud. There, on a hill, surrounded by trees, stands a new tribal building containing offices, classrooms, a gymnasium, and a kitchen.

New vitality was injected into tribal leadership after World War II with the Indian Claims Commission. The concept behind the commission, created by Congress in 1946, enabled any Indian tribe that believed it had been defrauded or wronged by the government, at any time in its history, to present its complaints. This invitation to the Kickapoo to regain some of their losses helped bring the tribe together and provided the leadership with a project. Eventually claims were prepared for all the lands the Kickapoo had relinquished. The case involving Illinois lands is still pending, but in the other decisions the court awarded payments of over $1,500,000 to the tribe.

The new direction in tribal leadership continued when in 1956 Paul White, tribal chairman, participated in a meeting that brought in assistance from the United States Public Health Service for the Kickapoo. Since that time a Community Health Representative works with several persons capable of speaking Kickapoo who can administer first aid and advise on nutrition and home nursing. If necessary they also provide transportation to neighboring hospitals and assist in communication when the patient speaks only the native language. The major health problems of the present time is diabetes and illness associated with inadequate, unbalanced diets, and impure water.

Another tribal chairman, James Wahpepah, took the initiative in the area of education. In 1965, he was instrumental in establishing the Kickapoo Head Start Program that accepted children of all races. Approximately one-half of the sixty children are Kickapoo and Indian awareness is being taught.

Since 1972, more government programs have been made available, including the Office of Native American Programs (ONAP) that trains people to write proposals for new projects and to manage the programs once they are funded. Most of these programs are directed toward the improvement of economic and educational levels.

The Maintenance Program, supported by the Indian Health Service, attempts to improve that aspect of housing that is related to health. A worker employed by the tribe repairs pumps and wells for better water supply and repairs and advises on the maintenance of sanitation facilities. Small charges are made for the service and full charges are made for the parts, in the hope that this program will function without subsidy.

Some assistance is provided through the Absentee Shawnee Housing Authority funded by the Department of Housing and Urban Development. Under the agreement the Kickapoo people are eligible for ten new houses per year provided that the recipient's income is under $4,500 a year and that he owns one and a quarter acre of land. The large lot is necessary for the installation of a septic system. The custom-built home costs approximately $17,500 but the price can be reduced by the owner through working up to four hundred hours on the project.

The Indian Action Team is supported by the Commissioner of Indian Affairs and teaches the construction trades, including carpentry, bricklaying, and plumbing. After one year of training, the student is assisted in finding suitable employment. Very often these men are employed by contractors building low-income homes.

Sharp contrast between the present Kickapoo and his fathers lies in education. In 1974, all of the 408 Kickapoo children between the ages of five and eighteen were enrolled in school. Most of them attended local schools although thirteen were in boarding schools. Forty per cent of the Kickapoo twenty-five years or older have completed high school, and that number is constantly increasing. Financial assistance is provided for Kickapoo to attend college and for those who choose to learn secretarial skills and how to work in health services. The Comprehensive Employment Training Act provides

GEORGE KISHKETON, Kickapoo leader and tribal chairman during the 1920's and 1930's.

support. The community building of the tribe is also the location for non-credit courses, such as Kickapoo arts and crafts and language training.

While very few of the Kickapoo farm, they are hard-working people. Many, from their homes in Oklahoma and Mexico, follow the harvests north during the summer and then return to their homes during the winter. Others work in the surrounding cities and many find employment at Tinker Air Force Base in Oklahoma City. They have scattered all over the United States in cities and farms in search of employment.

Even so the unemployment for the Kickapoo in recent years was approximately nineteen per cent while unemployment for the Lincoln County was under five per cent. Their per capita annual income was also lower, with the average for the Kickapoo in 1966 of $725 compared to an average in Pottawatomi County of $1,867. Economic upgrading of daily life remains one of the most important needs of the Kickapoo.

A problem unique to the Kickapoo is the matter of citizenship. Ever since Mackenzie forcibly returned a portion of the tribe to Oklahoma, there has been frequent visiting between the Oklahoma and Mexican groups. No restrictions have been placed on these tribal members as they cross the border, but neither has Congress specifically decided the status of the Kickapoo Indians who have been born in Mexico. All this is further complicated by the failure of the Kickapoo to register births with government offi-

TRIBAL BUILDING of the Kickapoo Tribe, McLoud, Oklahoma.

cials, and since they have not belonged to a Christian church, there is no record of baptism.

The problem of Kickapoo crossing the border is solved by the United States Immigration Service issuing a pass which identifies the person, not as an American or Mexican, but as a Kickapoo. This permits him to cross the border without restriction "pending clarification of status by Congress." A more serious injustice, however, arises when that person, who was born in Mexico or owns no record of birth, migrates to Oklahoma and applies for state welfare. State law makes this person ineligible; yet historically all Kickapoo belong to the United States.

Membership in religious bodies also reflects a basic change in the tribe. Approximately one-third are members of a Protestant Church, while another one-third subscribe to both Protestant and tribal faiths. Thirteen per cent are members of the Native American Church and only eleven per cent adhere completely and solely to the tribal faith. Most of the Protestants are found in the younger group; the Native American Church members are in the middle age group; and the tribal faith followers are in the older age group.

The use of the tribal language, like the tribal religions, is also declining. In 1974, only two children out of 173, who were under the age of thirteen, preferred Kickapoo to English. The majority of the people are bi-lingual, but the trend to English is strong. This trend may be reversed with the growing awareness of the Kickapoo heritage, and tribal leadership had made classes in the Kickapoo language available.

THE FUTURE

The future of the tribe lies within the province of the members themselves, but there are certain limitations which restrict their action. There is still a tension in the tribe between the traditionalists and the modernists, just as there is in many other societies. The future depends on the degree of cooperation the tribe can gain for its projects. Even though this tension exists, loyalty to each other is strong and mutual interests lead to unity. Both groups have accepted the ideas of education and assistance from the government and acknowledge the inevitability of change. The lifestyle of tribal members may be different but they are still Kickapoo.

The trend in tribal leadership is toward a greater role for the modernists. As more and more young people go to school and college, and travel over the United States in search of work, they will be assimilated into the American way of life. The future of the tribe looks bright because the median age is only eighteen, but it also means that the younger majority will make the decisions. Increasing communication with modern industrial society is the key. In the earlier century as the Kickapoo were isolated and only a few older males had contact with the white man, traditions could remain strong, but in the twentieth century, isolation, even for those who search for it, is hard to find.

Courtesy of George R. Nielsen

CHILDREN AT THE KICKAPOO HEADSTART SCHOOL. The school enrolls children of all races.

At the same time, there is a trend toward intermarriage between the Kickapoo and Native Americans of the neighboring areas. Because the number of eligible mates is limited in the Kickapoo community, more and more persons will marry outside their tribe. As other tribes have more rapidly adjusted than have the Kickapoo, loss of Kickapoo culture will be accelerated. The Kickapoo will continue to recognize their tribal ancestry and continue to be Native Americans, but fewer will be full-blooded Kickapoo.

Just as there is an increasing social interaction between the Kickapoo and the neighboring Native Americans, so will there be growing participation in larger organizational units such as the Central Tribes of the Shawnee (CTSA). Funding agencies are more receptive to requests from larger units, and the political influence wielded by a larger association is more impressive. The CTSA, composed of Kickapoo, Citizen Potawatomi and the Absentee Shawnee, already directs several of the federally sponsored programs.

The tribal leadership, through its Office of Economic Development Program (OEDP), has examined future possibilities for the tribe, especially in the economic sector, looking for a source of tribal income. The leaders have explored such possibilities as land acquisition in order to lure industry into their area and also the possibility of supporting a truck farm. Another possibility for service to the tribe would be a non-profit tribal store for their members.

94

Even though such projects may never develop, at least the leadership is striving to find ways to improve the economic life of the tribe.

The Kickapoo of the future will probably become more comfortable in American society and lose much of the tribal culture. He will become more like those Native Americans who have more readily assimilated. He will be a person who holds a job during the week amidst white workers, and then in the evenings and on weekends will participate with his family and friends in the preservation of those of his traditions which are not incompatible with industrial life. The task that remains for the Kickapoo will be to learn how to compete in contemporary society and yet maintain Kickapoo identity. The task that remains for contemporary society will be to study and appreciate that Kickapoo identity and recognize its unique contributions to America and to try to undo the long injustices of the past.

Courtesy of George R. Nielsen

CONTEMPORARY SUMMER HOUSE without the roof. The modern electrical farm lot light provides the contrast between traditional and modern ways of life.

SUGGESTED READING

The following works represent the best and most readily accessible studies of the Kickapoo. Other scholarly studies are available in articles and dissertations.

BUNTIN, MARTHA. "The Mexican Kickapoo," *Chronicles of Oklahoma*, XI (March-June, 1933), 691-708; 823-837.

The Kickapoo who lived in Oklahoma after 1874 were often called Mexican Kickapoo. The article is about the Kickapoo during the 1870's and 1880's, and examines their removal from Mexico and the problems they faced in their new home.

FOREMAN, GRANT. *Advancing the Frontier, 1830-1860*. Norman: University of Oklahoma Press, 1933.

A valuable study of the emigrant and resident Indians in Indian Territory.

_____ . *Last Trek of the Indians.* Chicago: University of Chicago Press, 1946.

Chapter XI deals with the Kickapoo Tribe.

GIBSON, A. M. *The Kickapoos: Lords of the Middle Border*. Norman: University of Oklahoma Press, 1963.

An excellent and comprehensive history of the Kickapoo from their Wisconsin days until 1920.

JABLOW, JOSEPH. *Indians of Illinois and Indiana*. New York: Garland Publishers, Inc., 1974.

A factual report of the Kickapoo as residents in Illinois and Indiana prepared originally for the Court of Claims.

RITZENTHALER, ROBERT E. and PETERSON, FREDERICK A. *The Mexican Kickapoo Indians. Publications in Anthropology* No. 2. Milwaukee: Milwaukee Public Museum, 1956.

An anthropological study of the Kickapoo as the result of a field visit in 1954.

GEORGE R. NIELSEN holds a Ph.D. from the University of Iowa and is associate professor of history at Concordia College, River Forest, Illinois. A native of Texas, he is interested primarily in ethnic history and 19th century America. Professor Nielsen served as assistant editor of the *Texas Indian Papers* and as a researcher for the Sac and Fox claims case. He has interviewed Native Americans for the American Indian Research Project at the University of South Dakota. A Fullbright scholar, Nielsen has recently completed the manuscript, "In Search of a Home: The Sorbs (Wends) on the Australian and Texas Frontiers."

KICKAPOO HISTORY

What any historian writes depends more upon the records available to him than his own personal research with living people when he summarizes events that span three and a half centuries. The very well qualified author of this volume necessarily had to interpret documents produced by literate Europeans or their descendants. Thus, these sources of information tend to express ingrained cultural biases.

A firm adherance to Kickapoo religious beliefs has motivated the nearly unique Kickapoo resistance to European domination, and enabled a core of Kickapoo culture to survive over three centuries of cultural aggression. Those who adhere to Kickapoo tribal belief may believe rather a different version of Kickapoo history than that expressed in this volume. They may conceive the world and its events in very different terms from those of the scientific Anglo-American historian. This volume does not pretend to interpret the Kickapoo historic experience in those Kickapoo cultural terms. It attempts only the best possible interpretation in terms of the ways of thought of Western Civilization.

John I. Griffin